Find
Learn
Become

A Poem By

Tommy

Sheffield

FIND LEARN BECOME
A POEM BY TOMMY SHEFFIELD

iUniverse books may be ordered through booksellers or by contacting:

iUniverse
1663 Liberty Drive
Bloomington, IN 47403
www.iuniverse.com
1-800-Authors (1-800-288-4677)

Because of the dynamic nature of the Internet, any web addresses or links contained in this book may have changed since publication and may no longer be valid. The views expressed in this work are solely those of the author and do not necessarily reflect the views of the publisher, and the publisher hereby disclaims any responsibility for them.

Any people depicted in stock imagery provided by Thinkstock are models,
and such images are being used for illustrative purposes only.
Certain stock imagery © Thinkstock.

ISBN: 978-1-4917-7518-9 (sc)
ISBN: 978-1-4917-7519-6 (e)

Library of Congress Control Number: 2015913348

Print information available on the last page.

iUniverse rev. date: 1/7/2016

for

Kevin Rowland

and

Joseph Mirenda

About the Text

The first draft of *Find Learn Become* originally developed from an idea I had after writing my first ever "word sharing" stanza, which uses one or two words to begin a stanza that then interweaves through itself to allow two simultaneous voices to speak (and often contradict each other) within one stanza. A short poem I wrote, titled "Infinite," should provide an example of what I mean:

$$\begin{array}{llll} & \text{duality} & \text{soul} & \\ \text{the} & \text{of one's} & & \text{is} \\ & \text{causality} & \text{mind} & \end{array}$$

This stanza/poem consists of eight words and is what I call an "infinite stanza"—a type of word sharing stanza that can be read over and over endlessly. Technically, it is meant to be read as "the duality of one's mind is the causality of one's soul"—but it can also be read (in a more rambling sort of way) as "the duality of one's mind is the causality of one's soul is the duality of one's mind is the causality of one's soul…" and so on. After discovering this technique, I spent three strange days handwriting the first draft of the manuscript for *Find Learn Become*, originally titled in my sporadic scrawl "A Song for the Dead." I then spent the next four years editing that manuscript. Thanks to my editors—my father Stephen Sheffield and my friends Danny Rathbun (*il miglior fabbro*) and Max Wollner—what I ended up with is what you hold in your hands. Read these.

Happiness is particular. Sadness is universal.

Find Learn Become

"What are the roots that clutch, what branches grow
Out of this stony rubbish? Son of man,
You cannot say, or guess, for you know only
A heap of broken images, where the sun beats,
And the dead tree gives no shelter, the cricket no relief,
And the dry stone no sound of water. Only
There is shadow under this red rock,
(Come in under the shadow of this red rock),
And I will show you something different from either
Your shadow at morning striding behind you
Or your shadow at evening rising to meet you;
I will show you fear in a handful of dust."

—T.S. Eliot,
The Waste Land

And the Lord said to Satan, "Whence do you come?"

And Satan answered the Lord, "From roaming the earth and patrolling it."

And the Lord said to Satan, "Have you noticed my servant Job, and that there is no one on earth like him, faultless and upright, fearing God and avoiding evil? He still holds fast to his innocence although you incited me against him to ruin him without cause."

And Satan answered the Lord and said, "Skin for skin! All that a man has will he give for his life. But now put forth your hand and touch his bone and his flesh, and surely he will blaspheme you to your face."

And the Lord said to Satan, "He is in your power; only spare his life."

—Job 2:2-6, NAB

I. Fire

                                    realize   mortal   life   pure.
And then it all happened, helping me to   the   man that I am. To me,   is
                                    feel like   terrible   death   wretched.

Burning skin turns raindrops tepid. This world is something I cannot endure.[1]

Man / Mine / Others / I / We / She / You / Marissa / They / Heather / Anne / Us

                    are all dying. Everyone is dying.

I live to be nothing   But who am I   I'm just a   A broken   Viciously   Laughably
more than my name.   to complain?   stain.   pane.   tame.   sane.

            are   forgotten   hopes
We   almost   our
    have   amongst   dreams

(Static.)   (Realization.)   (Denial.)

Look,   stands   much!   do you listen   hear   ?
        there   too   Oh, how   to   as it burns away in front of you
Where   again,   few!   it hurts   love   !

Come close to our folly.
_____

When   pyre   fight   all   to smile   while I   around him.
        a   must   for   things   at   wonderfully
Soon   man   light   good,   to gaze   die   look away.

"I am hurt." He gives me a lecture. "I feel pain." He gives me pills. Like you know
what it's like. There are no words left to express what is severe. We live in extremity.
We bask in longevity. Nothingness is a fearful imagination we avoid at all costs.
Surrounded with comforts, you know nothing of pain.

Now imagine your entire family, dying all at once.
Two kinds of love, severed to nothing.

I	sunlight	your	This fear,
think	through	lips to	its fingers
the	clouds	smile in	are gripped
world	and	its WAKE.	round my
of you	dusk.	UP. You,	chest, to
darling.	The	trembling	smother the
You	rain,	heartbeat,	love we
brought	it stopped	HOLD.	held stubborn
me	for	ON.	too long.

The lights of my life will be lost forever.

II. Mend

Chris,

I heard about the fire. Words cannot express how sorry I am for your loss. Your sister and I have readied the guest bedroom for you to come stay for as long as you need. We'll be by your side by tomorrow night at the latest, so hold tight until then. We've been praying every day for your speedy recovery. Your Mom put your family's name in the church prayer book, and Father Preston has offered to come visit you, if you'd like. Can't wait to see you.

Your brother-in-law,
Peter

A fragmentation of consciousness began my spiral. To let the wind, with its crisp deception, funnel me into enmity and madness. I had once thought, a couple years ago, that I had finally made it. I had braved the adolescent mystery and emerged victorious into adulthood. I had found love, however fleeting it was, and had even started going back to church, so my girls could brave the mystery better than I. My poor girls. You, incarnadine devil, slippery Satan; you, who ripped down the walls of my sanity, burned the temple of my faith, and cast my heart into conflagration—you will regret tempting my spirit; taunting my fervor. You dangled perfection before me, laughed in my face, and burned my heaven to the ground. How cruel. To leave a man alone in a world that turns, despite the deaths of his daughters, or his wife, the green majesty of nature itself reinforces the torment. Oh! To be alive is torment. To not have been taken in the fire. To have watched it. To have heard it. To have felt its red hot fingers, slicing through sizzling skin. I am a ghost among men, blind to the beauties of the world. I hang, from a fearful gallows, smothered and suffocated by the roped smoke of suffering. Below my feet, I see the rising flames, but this cruel world, which has hunted my idealism to extinction and wrenched the color from my vision, refuses to let me fade easily from existence. It has locked me in isolation, a ghost among men, floating alongside hearts that still hold passion, like a shirt at the dry cleaners: racked, rotating, repetitive, residual, and reminiscent of past humanity. I have nothing upon which I can place the blame, so I inherently blame myself.

(Struggle)(Rest)(Repeat)

The days pass without meaning. My sense of place and time blends into a confused conglomerate of memories I try to remember, and those I try to forget. Times, dates, all forgotten after the funeral.

	hold		love		alive		death		difficult.
I		true		is		and		is too	
	believe		he		a lie		life		easy.

I went to my bank to withdraw from the ATM.
I don't usually go into the bank; people tend to wince at my face.

15

Even so, I'd never have done different. Even if the interminable strength of the
entirety of the universe held my feet to the ground, I'd still have destroyed
my hands clawing at the earthen clay to halt my wife's screams.

      take   shivers   Remember?

Please   my   away   Good.

        warm   name   That's why it hurts.

We used to snuggle under the covers until the sea of our bodies settled to the still waters of sleep.

      tear   the world   today

a   in   of   outweighs

      care   the seam   tomorrow

                          [We know what makes us better.]

                          [We do what makes us worse.]

                                          till   lose them

                                Love   today   tomorrow.

                                  them   ends

                I   be

where   can't   a good day. *   And I'm beginning to lose track of what's real.

       there   have

                                            Forgive

point

                                    me   for

                                      asking

the

                                  but   what

                                  happens

                                  when   we

                                  die?

to

                          "You finally stretched your feet and
                    ghosted away from me, you had to fade away,
                  you had to leave, I'm pleading for one more time
               with what I know now, I'm begging for the same flake

16

to fall twice for the first time, I'm begging for what wasn't said.
That night the snow shaped the land, and I walked home,
I laughed the whole way because I suppose
if it hurts, it's worth it, but now that ghost is me."

I go,

—Pianos Become the Teeth,
"I'll Be Damned"

wherever

And shouldn't you be here, with me?

Or maybe here?

Because now

me

no   of your   around   one more.
    one   jokes   me   I live for those.
Just   makes   tell   anymore,

I miss them, yes, I miss them so.   follows

Each   caskets,   seats   they haunt   down.
    empty   three   in all,   me
These   seat,   caskets   they tear   thoroughly.

it

I   to   burnt
    watch   express   with
and   how   mine,
    I   it   my
wait   felt   clementine,   but
    and   to   spattered,
I   feel   blind,
    wish   her   seared in
for   flesh,   my mind;   pain
    a   absurd,   I must   from
word   melted;   look away

* If   mind
        you   don't   following
                                me
                            around
                            for a bit more
                                    I
                                like to
                        pace

17

                                                    when
                                                        their

                                                    faces
                                                        flood
                                                    my
                                                    mind;
forgive
my
        awkward demeanor,
my
        strange
lack
        of zest,

But I've lost all that.

Please,
        bear   time.
                with   last
            me   the
again,
                    for

        hopefully

                                        There
                                            well, see, no;
                            it was gone,
                                        for a moment,

                            but now it's come back.

        And   won't   I   come back,   is   love   shit.
                I   say   can't   someone   still   this
        But   must   they   believe   will   reading   face.

Thank you,   Still reading?   Please leave,
I welcome you   What are you, a sadist?   I never liked you
into my soul.   I fucking doubt it.   here with me anyway.

                love   you   given, but   a likeness.
        You don't   what   are   you've never felt
                know   comforts   until   lifelessness.

"My God. Look at him. The poor man. When he got home and realized his family was in the fire,
he ran into the house. The firefighters found him clutching his wife's burning corpse, if you can
believe it. See these markings here? You can actually see where her body rested in his arms."

III. Renunciation

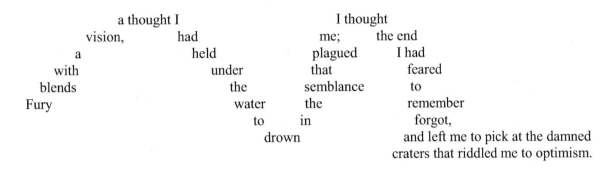

```
            a thought I                        I thought
    vision,       had              me;      the end
 a                held          plagued      I had
with            under          that          feared
blends            the          semblance     to
Fury            water          the           remember
                 to            in            forgot,
               drown                    and left me to pick at the damned
                                        craters that riddled me to optimism.
```

At the peak of sunset, Apollo is at home.
I am at home in my home alone and I think I've worsened from it.
I eat meals with the three chairs in which the empty coffins of my memory sit.
Nine thousand dead words in the tomb of this tome.

```
      day,     shade,    memory    loss
 the      its      the       of     follows
      night,   light,    mimicry   fire
```

I like to walk, through the park, but I keep from the playground.
The kids don't know how to react to my scars. And I'd rather avoid all that.

```
When                 back
     I    stepped    in
      first                that church
```

Even there,   They wouldn't   But that   My pain,   Interpreted by the   I can never smile
they   dare   baby   stamped all   most innocent   without creating a
stared   stare   that   over me,   of all to be   demented form of
     at   for   cried when   for all   grotesque,   my previous self;
me.   long.   looking at me. to see.   with which I agree. no mirrors,
                                                                                                no photographs,
                                                                                                no memories.

"This is lies, this is bullshit. I resolve you with a trick of hand and a joke of sight."

—Pg. 99,
"Hotel Nevada, 1982"

Cigarettes, whiskey, pot, painkillers, speed, coke, crack, meth, molly, ecstasy, horse tranquilizers, sniffed glues and gasolines, opium, acid, shrooms, salvia, peyote, DXM and the grape cough syrup that comes with it, PCP, heroin.

> In that order, lay my past
> two years. Even addiction
> couldn't keep me sober
> from their screams.

I synthesized Dipropanoyl morphine, a drug stronger than morphine and heroin, using propanic anhydride, a chemical unwatched by the DEA, to extract the substance, using a recipe I found on a forum written by an amateur who had admittedly researched using Wikipedia, and for about ten minutes, the heat that sweated my conscience, disguised by my creation, cooled to what I remember before the flames. I gambled with God that day but don't call me foolish for I knew my intent and the purpose of my risk was to ward off the remnants of my past that exist.

> Needless to say,
> the drug nor the risk imparted peace
> upon me.

That prosthetic nose. The one the doctor gave me to wear.
It itches with a repetition that would shame a hummingbird's wing.

Sometimes

when I think no one can see,
I take it off and scratch where my nose used to be.

One time

when I did, a dog nearby attacked the monster he saw,
protecting his owner from the stench of imperfection.

Every time

I see bodies, going places, through the streets, in the park, on the subway;
I notice they managed to keep from disfigurement, and for that, I applaud them.

No time

not once, has another commented on my looks.
To praise would be preposterous and to insult would be sadistic,
so instead it remains unspoken, as if I had no appearance at all.

I   am
                                         a   ghost
among   men

Floating, a bag of bones, burns, and blood, copying those around it for hope of camouflage in its natural environment. It has adapted to social difficulties with even more aptitude. While most people genuinely smile, and wave, and meet others gladly, this specimen has found a way to blend in soundly with short, finite conversations that shun the shy and weird out the outgoing. Not overtly abrasive, but distanced, distracted, as if nothing could garner its full attention.

I tried many times, over the course of this study, to revive his spirit. I told him the usual: "time heals all wounds," "God has a plan," "we're in this together," bullcrap.
    It's all bullcrap and bullhonkey.

        All the things they do to

make   you   better   seem

        to   make

                me

            worse.

        would say   am   sound   you saw me last,   leave me be,
You   I   more   when   can   *
    don't know that   sleep   than   my dreams   I have peace, please?

                instead of closure,   that   are gone.
        *but,   now   they
            it seems   I and   can't do that.

    Love's virginity tempted me to commitment, betrothal, and procreation.

It kept me close, slit my throat, and tossed me into the river.

    I will die a virgin to its majesty.

                    I reached into the clouds and ripped out their tears.

                    How foolish of me.

    They rained down on my soul, who, soaked in water, I hung to dry outside.
When the vicious winds, in all their glorious indifference, swept away the animus of my being,

            I was left, bereft, to walk this planet
            a ghost among men.

The corpse then stood up and looked at its hideous self in the mirror. It leaned in closely, kneading the edges of cauterization that plagued its complexion. It looked past the surface elements of its composition, down, deep into the marrow of its being to find an answer.

And the abyss, in its response, left him wanting.

The world was

done

with

you.

```
            gods        L                     K
   Can   humans         O    each other?      I    not  and
            animals     V    ?other each      L
                        E                     L
```

‡ think not.

Ha!   ‡deally.

‡ worry for you.

When Christmas came, the song I sang was wondrous.
Luckily, in my lonesome, the lyrical libeling laid heavily
on
me
alone.

Stark the feral mangled clings
Gory you the new torn king
Teeth from birth and worsely wild
Gods and sinners reconciled.

Sinful, all ye nations surmise
Coin the style of the rise
With the pandemic roast for shame
Christ is adorned in restless maim
Stark the feral mangled clings
Gory you the new torn king.

You're the one we call God?

Have we met before?

I feel you've seen my face once, maybe

twice before.

I'd been meaning to ask you, and if you don't have the time to listen, I understand, but,
well, you kind of left me hanging there, from that noose you roped me into?
Ah, you probably don't remember.

Well

anyways   I was

wondering

you've seen all, know all, every aspect of the galaxy is your dominion, and I was wondering,
well, this wasteland you called the world, did you create this to taunt me?

Is the only reason I'm alive to concentrate

on horrible paintings that press   until the greatest surge of
wet through my eyes? I audiate   rationalization crashes over
my madness, within the bounds   my partially haired scalp;
of infinity I explore all ends. But   we, the dead, are buried.
they, like I, are weak; mortality
creeps on their shoulders

And in a dream that later woke me with a dark reeling,
we   sun   wastefully   treading
     the   play   alone   softly
see   gun   gracefully   floating
     the   of which   heavens   sadly   fell.
be   one   the   better
     the   and   stars of   night
me   moon   I;   dying
I watched my shadow bury graves on an ethereal ceiling.

It had been a long day at the office and by the end of it I felt thinner than thread. I used to get
beers after work with some of the other writers but they stopped inviting me as of late.
The rain was nice enough to accompany me on my walk home.

The
lord
works
in mysterious
ways

              night   can
If I go out at   people   see
              day   can't

Forever lovely, thoughtful, understanding, kindhearted; please avert your eyes.

Thick raindrops dropping on a burning rooftop
Spit spat spattering like acid tear drops
That drip down into dirty gutters
And weave over and under
Themselves with a soft
And agonizing dribble.

Beneath panicked feet the
Mud is splish splash splattering
The puddles are squish squash scattering
Damp drowned soil, smothering
Moisture from the rain.

Gasp, pant, wheeze
Mouths struggling to breathe
Like fish gulping for their feed
We are wet and worn and above us
Thunder is looming and
With loud bangs, booming
Cratch! The rigid light vein stretches
Down into the grass and beckons
Fire bleed from where indeed
The lightning stabbed the ground.

Crackle! Sparks and embers!
A cheerful dance of heated splendor
Quickly becomes an inferno
That waltzes without mercy.

Snap! goes the house's back
It falls, its spine twists, and hits
The ground and is soon
Engulfed in the rising flames.

Slowly   horrible   to be
    I find these   bouts   enticing.
For   explosive   of insanity

V. Adjustment

I've been living
with Peter and Kelsey
for a month now.
They are good, kind people.
They make me breakfast in the morning.
I sit on the back porch and watch the clouds
and play fetch with the neighbor's dog. I
pace with a ceaseless gait, "Watch the ugly
man scratch his face." I will not be their
jester. I will not be their clown. My hair,
it pokes out like a hideous crown—
I'm the king of this town.

They will look past their eyes
to find a heart beneath these binds.
If they look to me and scowl,
they are merely others, most
unworthy of my growl.

What is that
Motherfucker looks like E.T.
Must be a moloch
"It came from a swamp"

Parasitic laughter be not my bane.

Each day, one brick stacks beside me,

Forming around me a sort of shield

The candles I've lit have kept burning—
no more:
I douse their disaster with spit I've held close for what feels like a century.

And the day approaches,
but in my insistently inconsistent thoughts,
I am at home in blind sleep.

I have looked
away
from my reflection
more
times than I can
count

"Shouldn't you be going to school?"

"I swear daddy, we're both sick."

"If I don't tell Mom, will you two promise you won't look for your presents this Christmas?

Because

we've run out of places to hide them."

Thank God, that house and that family are gone, now the ashes that remain can scatter and blend
so that not even a bone from my girls could be found until the ceiling was picked off the ground.

You are a ghost among men. Even now the people act like they can't see you.

When deep down they know that at first glance, when they saw me,
they looked at their feet, as if I were naked, or making a scene.

As I was saying, a ghost among men,
trapped in the void of immortality,
and your revival is soon.

VI. MANIFESTIVAL

"He who makes a beast of himself gets rid of the pain of being a man."
—Dr. Johnson

PART 1: THE FEARED REALITY

White   Radiant words   Mumbling
Lights   Trembling   Greatness
    Whispers   Darkness shining   Among the imagined sunset
                                             Whose deception set upon me
                                             And seemed grace
                                             Denied me indifference.
                               I've waited for too long to see these
                                             Memories gone—
           Wondrous   But they are constant.
         Inconceivable
          Dangerous   Latching onto the depths of my chest
           Believable   They are insulting to my intellect
A confidence, stretching around me   Most of which is gone.

It was simply complicated
So many things wrong
That everything seemed right.

                                     Something in me doubts it.
    "What are you, on drugs?"   Who are we to stumble into living?
                         Born without a choice we are bred to die.
Or perhaps it isn't that way
                           judgment
             Maybe all the   they're talking about is within ourselves
                   salvation

Maybe they were all metaphors—maybe heaven is a just and moral earth; maybe purgatory really means that we just die over and over, reincarnating until our souls are ready for heaven; and maybe hell is a metaphor for being stuck on earth, damned to keep dying until the end of everything.

No, that's insane.   Is it?   Yes.

WHO ARE YOU TO JUDGE WHAT YOU DON'T KNOW

Says the one, who knows nothing.

         Well I wouldn't say I know nothing, I think everything is a more charming fit.
Why so extreme?

                                         I revel in extremity.
How's that going for you?

                                     I appear happy to others.
That's all that matters.

We cannot decide between ourselves and nightly demons who is more wretched and filthy.

We've achieved nothing but trivial excess and our souls are still hurting.

Could we be called the saviors?
Doubtful.

For we are the demons that plague this world
We are the crushers and destroyers unfurled
We fill the graveyards, we make the dead:
When we can't kill ourselves,
We kill someone else instead.

Better they die, than we learn to like them.
Better they die, because then we'll get to fight them.
Better they die.

I think you're being nihilistic.

I like to think of myself as a critic.

But critics don't know shit.

They look at the shit,
They touch the shit,
But they can't take the shit.

Now you're being crude.

Nope. Just rude.

Why can't we suffer from here on out?

We've allowed a new Martyrdom—
Let us revel in its absurdity.

Why can't we kill them all,
And burn all their cities?

You can't kill everyone.

I beg to differ.

Our martyrs are murderers,
Murdered for murder's sake.
Carvers and caterers,
Who's going to cut the cake?

I've never seemed more incredibly inane.

Add an s to that and I'd feel the same.

PART 2: JUSTICE

Trust us
We control your safety
We control your brain
We are empty minds
You are all insane.

Broken knuckles, handcuffed wrists,
Bloody hands now clenched to fists.

Here, take this experimental medication,
We'd like to record your pain.

Is there anything I can do instead?

Only if you'd rather be dead.

I hear voices

How do I know you're telling the truth?
You show a good amount of resilience to them.

If I act like I'm hearing voices, would you prefer that?

Well, yes.

Good thing you're controlling my medicine,
Causeyoudontknowwhatthefuckyouretalkingabout.

I take offense at that notion.

Good to know you're more sensitive, less potent.

I believe you should leave.

A childish mind has durable mystique;
It protects the wealthy, it protects the weak.

Now that, I think, is rather steep.

Our immaturity has reached its peak.

Grant   souls,   find myself
   me   of   take   I'm   I'll   waiting
     one   You,   realm   me   where   make   to shine brightly.
      wish   great   down   you'd   use
       oh   love   below your   always   of
    exist,   God   of   eye   been,   this
     not   this   mine,   fair,   line,   you're   sunset,
   does   place   ever   you should   where   I'll
This place   does   fine.   know you're   I'll   make
        not   never mine.   never be.   use of
      exist.   this
                                          feast,

well it seems now that I'm the beast.

Please show a means to this peace.

Not a preacher? Not a priest?

Nay, I'm but a straggler in my life's crease.

Then let's make this poem a bit more brief.

PART 3: ARGUMENTAL

By choosing to be objective, you are subjectively objecting to the object of truth.

By choosing to be subjective, you are objectively subjecting to the subject of a lie.

Don't be a dick.

So says the prick.

Is your mind sick?

Why? You want a lick?

We have a sense of honor and now it seems to work toward stubborn minds and unflinching resolve: we take stands to save nothing and call attention to brief moments in meaninglessness— short memories of what you were thinking when a brink tinkered with your link to reality.

```
I'll                    I              you. How   I'm  This        worse. ? ? ?
   never              if  do              on   could not  is       and  ?     ?
      admit    and       it'll   mistake     You are mine  getting worse   ? ?
         that   wrong     be      the        do    ?          I         ?
            I'm          by blaming          that  Nope.      agree.    ?
                                                                        ?
```

I'm getting
More and more disturbed
By the number of times
I've been perturbed
By forces beyond my control
And I feel like it's building up
Inside me
I feel like it's growing

Within a heart of darkness
There is the dust of death
Sprinkled over
The ventricles and arteries
A lack of life
Flowing through my veins

And those voices
Those mouths that speak
They make me horrid
They call me a freak
Until all patience thins
Like the blood of the weak
Flowing quietly
Through a dead creek.

33

PART 4: TEMPTATION NATION

The wink of a care is all that remains.
Throw a few bucks, pity a few names;
Little by little, with little pertained,
We like to keep all things the same.

We smile and wave
In an effort to appear saintly;
We feast on angels' wings
As the sky whispers faintly:

"Government, oh government,
Who really are they dying for?"

Complexities and perplexities
(Questions galore),

Answers are the death of me:

drink
Let's whine some more.
fuck

There are resolving recountabilities revolving the raptures
that rape at the ridges of a soul's plaster.

It's for the good of the country!

What the fuck's a country?

You know, the nation!

What's that?

It's like, a collection of people that form a government.

And what's a government?

It's this thing that people made to keep everyone safe.

But for the majority of man's existence, those weren't around, right?

Precisely.

And yet, countries claim self-evidence in their right to power?

Correct.

Even though man lived for thousands of years without government?

Right.

And then man created government, yes?

Absolutely. Thank goodness he did.

Right.

So the government's claim to self-evidence is despite the fact that there is
significant evidence that man doesn't need government to survive, correct?

Yes, you could say that.

And if I were to live in the woods somewhere in America,
And claim that where I chose to live was my country,
I wouldn't have to pay taxes, go on probation,
Or go to jail for laws that are morally confused, right?

                            Mmhmm. But I don't see where you're going with this.

Precisely.

                  That terrible territory.
                  This cuff of a country.
                  If we expect a criminal
                    To break the law,
                      He will.
                      If we
                      Expect
                  The human race
                  To be falsely ideal,
                  Think again. We're
                  Nowhere close to
                    Being kempt.

PART 5: ENTROPY

Jesters and clowns
Filling the towns
Ending the prouder parts
Of being free:
I'd welcome them, would they welcome me?
What if they don't like me?
Am I good enough?
But they: they are superb!
How can I measure to their nerve?
How can I come close to knowing
Anything but nothing?
How can anyone?
We are forgetful ancestors of smarter men
We are the seed of a seething breed
Waiting on wants and neglecting true needs
God, I hope you agree
This world is a tree
That we are hacking at
Slowly—
We tear at its woody flesh
We trip its legacy
We slice at it
With drills and bombs and poisons and pains
We sever its veins
We bleed it till it stains
And then we wonder why
People bring guns to school
People blow up towers
People die in fires
People rape sons and daughters
People kill mothers and fathers
We wonder why.
We wonder, oh God! Why?
How could they do that?
But really, we shrug it off.
We shrug it off and hope
That it will never happen again.
But it will.
And it will keep happening.
And when you think it will stop happening,
It will happen again.
And I promise you,
By the end,
You'll want,
Oh God!
You'll wish,
For peace.

So while you're sitting there, in your small little chair, wondering where, oh God where

                                                            is
                                                            my
                                                            place
                                                            in
                                                            this
                                                            universe?

What the fuck am I doing here?
Why am I, day after day,
Stricken with fear?
Am I here to be afraid?
Am I here to be afraid?!?

OH GOD TELL ME PLEASE TELL ME OH GOD PLEASE TELL ME OH GOD PLEASE HAVE

MERCY

ON

ME.

PART 6: THE VEIN

Splits
Carrying away
Droplets
Of humanity
The people
They wonder
They sit there and think:
Why am I sad?
It's because
We're sitting there
Trying to reason
About why our life
Has been worthwhile,
Why what we've done
Is worth smiling about;
And what happens then
Is we think hard of all the things
That have panged at our chest,
All the things that made us feel
Like a sad and worthless mess,
Of the few places we've been,
Of everyone we've met,
Of everyone we've fucked,
And we wonder:
Why, oh my, *why?*
Why am I still here today?
Why haven't I died in some strange accident?
Lost to a blunted circumstance that enacted my life's fear
Years before I could learn to love the earth?
It's because your time on earth is not yet finished.
Live your life, for God's sake, live your life.
Humans were not meant to be caged.

PART 7: IMAGINATIONS, DYING

We haven't got much time

           Here on this place

                         We are running on empty

        The world's having trouble keeping up

And we are speeding ahead and away

               Rolling along:
               And hopefully—
               Someday—
            Someone will love me.

Someone will see my face, and they won't laugh at it.
They won't think of the things they've heard about me,
They won't look to their friends and smirk—
They'll look at the words I've left
On these few pages
And see themselves in me;
They'll find between us something same.
Maybe, someday,
Someone will smile when they hear my name.

                       You, you, you—you are my brother.
                          You too! You're my sister!
                       You all! You're all my family,
                          And I love you.

             Sure, there are some differences
                Between our lives;
           But we are all after the same things.
              We all want to be happy,
              We all want to be safe.

Suffering—please, please go away.

If it doesn't, it will. We have to be sad. We have to be.
If we didn't get sad—
If our emotions became more
Than constant fads—
Then what would happiness be?
Just another sadness for free?
What is a smile without envy?
What is an anger without patience?
I'd like to know, why dontcha tell me?
"'Cause kid, sometimes even the grownups don't know the answer."
But what if I find the answer? What if I figure it out?
"Well, I'd say you'd get a Nobel Prize or something of the sort."

No way. That's impossible. They wouldn't give that to me.
"Hey, don't say that. Nothing's impossible."

In your little head,
There are thousands of unopened doors.
There exists the potential
For the improvement
Of all mankind.
Think of the greatness we could accomplish.
And this greatness is not wealth,
It is not prestige,
It is not the price of a car,
Or the size of a television—
No, these things are not great.
They are merely comforts we've created
To coddle our creative courage.
And so what really matters,
What is really great,
Is that when given the chance
To improve the world
By helping others,
We do.
And when given the chance
To better ourselves—
We don't hesitate,
We don't make excuses:
We dig down deep inside
The shelter of our imagined egos
And find that certain courage
That's waiting for us,
And use it to change ourselves
Into something *more*.

PART 8: SENSELESS

The trickling springs
  That Winter brings
    Are how nature sings.

Her soul is all strewn
  Across the earth
    Among the green
    Yet rarely is she seen.

Her tranquil absence
  Is the saddest silence
    For we are trembling in her heartlands
    And we are fearful of what comes after

And maybe if we heard her voice,
Maybe if she spoke to us,
Her quiet words would help us learn
The beauty of a modest life,
The strength of an honest day.

There is water, flowing, under this bridge.
Look: the water—it's flowing!
I wish I could be that water.
I wish I could be something as beautiful
As what I've always imagined.
But I can't. I am only myself,
And I view it like a disease:
I long for the qualities of others,
I wish for everything but me;
For all but this debris.

But why oh why, Chris, why?
You are the only one for me.
You should feel weightless
You should feel peace
I love you, and you should love me.

How could you possibly love this?
What of me is living?
What of me is free?
I am merely waiting
For the cusp of mortality
To throw me in the sea,
And all I've got
Are my hopes and dreams with me.

So what I'm saying is,
When you say,
"Why am I sad?"
I will always answer:

It's because you were meant for something more,
And right now,
That room you're in has got a door,
And really,
You've got to open it,
And see what else your life
Is holding in store.

But I'm afraid. I'm scared of what comes next. There's darkness in this room and if I open the door
it will escape and leave me alone forever. I can't be alone forever. I can't be on my own.
The world is too large and I'm too small and I feel like a little kid at the mall
and I'm trying to run and catch up but all I can do is fall.

How do you think God felt, before there was an Earth?
And how do you think God felt,
When all we did was hurt?
How do you think God feels,
Every time we blow up an abortion clinic?
Every time we blow up an embassy?
Every time we willingly kill,
And each time we die—
How do you think God feels
When death consumes our lives?

PART 9: CRISP DARKNESS/SUNRISE

Like the flick of a light switch
There was a rush of shattered brightness
Swerving, with marvelous colors
That wrapped around images
Of my life's likeness—
Warming the soft surface of my skin.
And my eyes,
Adjusted to dusk,
Were born anew:
Under the soft and rising sun—
My heart beat faster,
A steady quickening,
Until my skin prickled,
And euphoria clothed me in confidence,
And I felt,
For the first time ever,
Like I was alive,
And that there was a hope,
Somewhere in me,
For redemption—
Not just my own,
But also the world's,
And its many people,
Coming together,
And joining hands,
And shining sunlight on the darkness
That ravages our loving minds.

> For we are not monsters
> We are not gods
> We are merely human beings
> And we have only just begun.

PART 10: VALEDICTION

In all my travels,
I have been but one place.
In all my learning,
I have learned but one thing.

We are a holy remembrance of a better time that never existed and a better place that has never been
and I feel like the one thing we can do to remedy this is to better ourselves. I feel like if we try, if
we go out of our way, we could dawn on a new day. I think we are the solution. I think we are
what is missing in the world. We: the compassionate, the understanding, the empathetic,
the knowing, the trustworthy, the honest, the modest, the pure,
the thoughtful—
that is who we aren't,
and that is who we need to be.

Not some vicious, unloving thing.

VII. Finding

Chris,

You say to me you cannot have a good day. I implore you to seek elsewhere than within.
The human mind is a dangerous place. Look without:

Peace is found outside yourself:

In what you do, what you enjoy, what you find rewarding, or how you conquer a challenge—

You are not meant to withhold forever.

You are allowed to laugh, be merry, meet the smiles of others even it means forcing it;
for you are a creature of love, and if love flows
through your actions and deeds and decisions and sacrifices,
you will earn the comfort of others.

Others.

People who can accept you.

They are out there, waiting.

Find solace in shallow thoughts,
they pleasure your monotony;
beauties on the TV:
they have *nothing* on me.

Look at the way my skin roughs along—
to me, it seems worthy of song.

Strength has eluded you
for a while now.
I hope you'll reach a point where
you can smile now.

Relax. Let the sides
of your mouth raise to a curl.

I promise, this will pass.

There are things we can't change.

It seems easy to come to terms with experiences apart from our own—

we can't force people to think like we think,

see like we see,

or

do like we do.

The green in the leaves of the trees agrees
that we may need to see things
in a different light—
through a lens that tints less.

But we are dependent on poison.

We pump it through our veins.

Never altogether unless you truly know you can better
the distance between yourself and whether
or not you do right or wrong.

Goodness knows excessive excess leads to excessiveness.

Don't try to please everyone,
you'll frustrate yourself.

And that whole thing you do with assuming the world is out to get you, it's falsely contrived.

"The world isn't against you, my dear, it just doesn't care."

—Modern Life is War,
"Marshalltown"

You are not what you eat,
you are where your feet
have traversed,
where your eyes have gazed,
your tongue has tasted,
your ears have heard,
your heart is wasted?

Now that's absurd.

You are yourself, your own, and only you have that.

"Someone may say it's good, but I'll never believe them.
The truth of its beauty has been lost by my senses."

—You,
whenever you said it.

Fuck that, man.

Make your heart an open house. Let those feelings you've been hiding
away be shared with those you've earned and those you trust—
they're more compassionate than you think.

Some people are just shy, others are insecure, others are anxious;
people are inherently good when the life they live allows them to be.

There are exceptions to every rule, there are constants and constellations which
we've never heard of, forces and physics holding it all together, and for what?

Chaos and heartbreak?

You are more beautiful than your exceptional mind has ever comprehended,
and even when you said you were a ghost among men, I believed you,

and it frightened me.

You, sir, are a miracle incarnate.

VIII. Learning

"Hello and welcome back to WHSV News 3.
In today's top story, a local man in Rockingham County is on a mission:
To improve his community, one house at a time.
Bernard Gordon is in Harrisonburg with Mr. Evans—over to you Bernard."

"Thanks Kelly.
Now, I'm here with Chris Nash, a Harrisonburg native.
He's been posting fliers and ads around town,
offering free construction aid to any local families in need of it.
So Chris, tell me, what did you do before working on houses?"

"I wrote. I, uh—I was a writer."

"What inspired you to teach yourself construction?"

"My wife and daughters,
they…they died.
In a fire.
I was burnt, in the fire.
That's why my face looks like it does.
After I lost my home,
I found that helping other people build theirs
was the only way to make myself feel better."

"And what about your hands?
Don't they hurt from the work?"

"They do, but I'm, um…I'm used to it."

"Here, look closer with the camera.
Can you see? Good.
Listen Chris,
I'm going to give you
all the money in my wallet—"

"No, really. I don't want it."

"Oh come on now.
There's forty bucks in there,
and you are going to take it
because you've earned it."

"Well…all right. But so you know,
I'll probably just donate it to the—"

"Amazing. You really are a giver aren't you Chris?
Well it's truly inspirational, to say the least.
We have to go—was there
anything else you wanted to say?"

"Yeah. The world's a nice place,
it's a shame we can't keep it that way."

Or can we? Ha! Idealism.

Maybe once this world we "own" gets sung the song of death, maybe it can feel a little better.

Maybe we'll see through the money, through the bullshit, there's terror out there—
it's cutting goodness into cutlets of meat to be sold
at a meatpacking plant so that the hungry can starve, securely.

Lest the richer world be only slightly inconvenienced by their suffering.

You, clever and swift, avoided your hardships.
With guile and control you made reality your own—

an impossible thought.

(If these walls could speak they'd be screaming:
We laugh at the things that make us sad, for they merely tried to bring us down.)

So I applaud you, and those who felt themselves through you,
for you are my harbinger of hope,
my prince of peace:
you are myself
and
you are others;
you are the tastes, the smells, the sights, the sounds—

I feel you're quite fitting to consider a complete success.

Death made his deal with you. If you braved the fire, and returned
those screams to several moments of happiness, you would be given a challenge:

To try, to attempt things you thought you couldn't do, to be surprised by what you could
accomplish. To give love to those who need it more than others, like the elderly, the disabled,
the disfigured, the ignored edges of society's embrace, those who stand out in a crowd;

(You, who wrong them and belittle them,
your concept of appearance disgusts me.)

to treat people the way you'd want to be treated, and to find reward in your mercy.

50

"People are people, regardless of anything."

—Andrew Jackson Jihad,
"People"

No matter what clips at the heels of our progress, it can be shaken off.

We,
the lifeless ghosts,
who parade through reality
with thoughts of lessened self-worth,
rejoice.

We are the chorus of collaboration,
whose hands join freely in pursuit of better life on earth.

He brought me aside.
"You know you're a good man, don't you?
What you're doing, helping people like you have been,
well—well it's a damn good thing. You hold your head high.
Nobody deserves to more." Isaac always liked to make me feel welcome.
We walked down past the bridge into the creek, taking off our shoes and sitting
with our feet in the water.

It was a beautiful day.

All around us, there are indications of humanity's brilliance:

To learn that a man with one leg climbed the tallest mountain in the world—

yeah, that inspired me.

To find that no matter how hard I try, my mom will always be a better person than me—

yeah, that drives me.

To have a gun pulled on me for driving 50 mph on a 40 mph street—

yeah, that jaded me.

We are each other.
We are everyone.
We are a collectivized consciousness
of experience and existence
that pulls and pushes at the
nearest nonsense we use as an excuse.

Lie to yourself.
Tell yourself you're great,
even if you don't agree with the claim.
Your future self will thank you kindly.

To do the opposite is to promote weakness in determination, to empty
our courage into the river to drown. No, we are capable of so much more.

Find Learn Become

It's scary to think I could never have learned to play anything on the guitar.
For an hour a week at the least, I derive self-satisfaction through creation
(who is my muse, my mask, my song, my love; creation is me),
and I highly suggest you try it.

Learn an instrument you thought you couldn't play, because you really can play it.
Learn to throw a frisbee, keep a journal, paint a portrait, start a business, write a poem,
cook, sing, sing till your neighbors bang on your apartment's wall,
then sing some more.

Sing a song for the dead.

After the torchlight red on sweaty faces
After the frosty silence in the gardens
After the agony in stony places
The shouting and the crying
Prison and palace and reverberation
Of thunder of spring over distant mountains
He who was living is now dead
We who were living are now dying
With a little patience

In this decayed hole among the mountains
In the faint moonlight, the grass is singing
Over the tumbled graves, about the chapel
There is the empty chapel, only the wind's home.
It has no windows, and the door swings,
Dry bones can harm no one.
Only a cock stood on the rooftree
Co co rico co co rico
In a flash of lightning. Then a damp gust
Bringing rain

Ganga was sunken, and the limp leaves
Waited for rain, while the black clouds
Gathered far distant, over Himavant.
The jungle crouched, humped in silence.
Then spoke the thunder[:][2]

   "Do not stand at my grave and weep,
   I am not there; I do not sleep.
   I am a thousand winds that blow,
   I am the diamond glints on snow,
   I am the sunlight on ripened grain,
   I am the gentle autumn rain.

When you awaken in the morning's hush
I am the swift uplifting rush
Of quiet birds in circled flight.
I am the soft stars that shine at night.
Do not stand at my grave and cry,
I am not here; I did not die." [3]

For in death, life's value is found.
The boredom of immortality would stain our thirst for life.
We are better, shorter, where the world's more beautiful.

IX. Becoming

We, succinct and brave,
we who wade through the waters
and wander the broken soil of the earth:

We are the strength.

There is nothing we can't do to preserve our humanity.

Merely be human,

do what humans do,

but when it comes down to it,

breathe deeply, and feel the world with your fingertips.

And then I learned the guitar, when I thought it was impossible (with my hands the way they
are), I met Simon Phillips, who taught me to think about music with an open, learning ear
and to slow things down for a bit; I tend to overdo dynamics and the parts I play
blend together, but to me, the conductor of infinite symphonies, my music,
though repetitive and wild and atonal and weird, it's *my* music:—
And that made all the difference to me.

I remember when I finally got the courage to play in front of people. The song I played wasn't
impressive. The sound of my singing voice must have been awful. My fingers slipped off the
frets a few too many times and one of my strings broke. But the small crowd ignored the
weakness in my appearance. They ignored the flaws in my musicianship. They merely
listened, and at the end, they congratulated my attempt with sincerity.

(Improve)(Rest)(Repeat)

I've been volunteering at a local Glenwood Springs nursing home for a short while now,
and yesterday, which was Valentine's Day, I was assigned to hand out tiny paper hearts
addressed to all the men and women in each room of every hallway in the building.
Each individual was grateful and, for the most part, indifferent to my appearance.

Please forgive my flaws, I swear they weren't here before.

Forgiven and forgotten, flaws are fairy tales to me.

We should value them even, for it is from them
that the aesthetic is traced—in them, we know ourselves.

We are experience.

We

should

experience

together,

what

the

end

holds

in

store.

And then I met Elden Majors, and he believed in me, and I believed him, to the point where when I told him I couldn't hear pitch, he said:

"Oh, come on. Of course you can."

And that has made all the difference.

We peruse the empty sea
in search of ourselves;
but we are lost.
Misguided, perhaps.
And with the sheets of the covers
of the beds you grew up in,

you shielded fear away.
Now you're old enough today
to find your own way.

Your destiny is confined to your actions.
It is by our choice decided.

Find, Learn, Become

Chris found something that meant something to him.
He found his talents in construction—gained from having
tried in vain to repair the skeletal remains of his family's home—
translated wonderfully to charity (through sadness comes empathy).

[We worlds, we are crumbling, collapsing on the clever irony of fate.]

He pursued something that meant the world to him, and he achieved it.

Have you?

I know I haven't. Not yet.

But idealism's unrealism creates doubt in educated hope; for this we must excuse ourselves.

Human lives are precious.

And therefore we should dedicate our lives
to an endearing prospect of victory in self-betterment.

Be at peace with weakness;
it is through ourselves that the good world shines.

There is no obstacle in the night's sleep
that our conscience can't sort through at daybreak.

"We echo in our haunted words. The strings are fire, the bass is roaring, the beat carries us on. If our bodies weave into the ground that they stand on they cannot fall down. As we slowly push the earth into itself it collapses us and we take photos to remember how great it was to be children or forgotten faces in the backgrounds of your lives. We've all been relatives or coworkers. We've all been forgiven. As we slowly push the earth into itself, it collapses us and we take photos. The song plays on but the record is cracking. The house is dark, all of the floors are creaking."

—The World is a Beautiful Place
and I am No Longer Afraid to Die,
"I Will Be Okay. Everything."

The oyster is our world, and through the outer shell that protects us, within the guard of darkness, when opened and examined, we find inside the earth the pearls of our selves we thought were gone.

Inside is you, the tender individual, whose choice it is to make light of your mortality.

Embrace your humanity.

Find, Learn, Become.

"I used to listen to my life,
I was so put together,
I chose what I wanted to be in that age of chasing sand,
the age of believing in everything,
but I couldn't save you,
I couldn't save what was taken away,
and I'm still singing, and you still can't stay.
You 'loved life,' and those words have lasted,
I just wish I would have had ears for more than what you said
because I still feel the lack long after.
Such a light body, such a quiet gait leaving behind the weight of the world,
I'll always think it was too early to lose your shine,
I guess the means that ends us means nothing,
I just hope it's the peace we all need,
Because I could love and drown in your God damned smile lines,
but I think I burnt up watching you rallying to stay alive,
and I guess that's fine.
It seems we all get sick,
we all die in some no name hospital with the same colored walls,
and I guess that's fine,
but I want to swallow, I want to stomach, I want to live.
It's been a rough while and some days are worse than others,
there's no proper way to feel, no mirth, no levity, no amazing grace,
just a flame on a lake floating away,
I can't let you lay,
I want you to know, I'm learning patience against my will,
I want you to know, I'll get by, always barely scraping
with just a hunger, with just a heart apart,
it's a hell of a thing."

—Pianos Become the Teeth,
"I'll Get By"

[1] This should be read as: "And then it all happened, helping me to realize the terrible man that I am. To me, life is wretched. Burning skin turns raindrops tepid." and "And then it all happened, helping me to feel like the mortal man that I am. To me, death is pure. This world is something I cannot endure."

[2] Excerpted from Section V ("What the Thunder Said") of *The Waste Land* by T.S. Eliot.

[3] "Do Not Stand at My Grave and Weep" by Mary Elizabeth Frye.

Acknowledgments

"Nothing of me is original. I am the combined effort of everybody I've ever known."

—Chuck Palahniuk, *Invisible Monsters*

I would like to thank everyone who contributed to the making of this book. This includes but is not limited to: my parents Stephen (editor) and Maureen Sheffield, my siblings Matt, Julia (and her husband Luke Lagacé and his family), and Paul Sheffield; Dennis and Peggy Sheffield, Bill and Pauline O'Rourke and all their wonderful children and grandchildren—Sean especially, for all the help and encouragement—and great-grandchildren, Victoria and Howard Pyle, Uncle Bobby; my close friend Danny Rathbun (primary editor); Dorian Delpopolo-Mills (front cover artist) and his family; Max (editor), Genni (artist), and Marc Wollner; Isaac, Jared, and the Rank family; Patrick, Dylan, Charlette, and the Callahan family; Alex Parker and the Parker family; Nic Mirenda and the Mirenda family; the Rowland family; Joseph Balzarett, Stephen Chastain, Peter Michel, Trish Seidel, Luke Nicastro, Brian Wood, Will Studabaker; Gus Caldwell, John Crogan, Josh Niezgoda, Brian Russo, and the Kilgore Trout family; Tierney Bates-Pineda, Austin Scarbel, Andrew Puffenbarger, Ryan Wisgerhof, Kyle Mctague; Jordan, Skyler, and the Daché family; Graham Farr and his family; Matt Evans, Chris West, Tim Blair, TJ Pickler, Billy Jenkins, Jun Cho, Ryan Wolter, Ryan Saba, Andrew Rowe, Geoff Craz, Derek Guzman, Andrew Brammer, Chris Bare; Justin, Dylan, and the Beveridge family; Derek Barry, Tyler Truitt, Sam Denny, Tyler Wallace, Taylor Gordon, Robert Byrnes (my boy), Raleigh Heckel, Alex Johnson, Daniel Oliver, Tom Barnes; Richard Aguilar, Nathan Irving and the Irving family, Terence Edelman, Matt McDermott; Edd Nawabi, Travis Brown, Rich Harriott, Stuart Taylor, Mike Lee, Matt Madison, Ryan Sacco, Chris Wren, David Winters, Mike Myers, Billy Byers, Ben Miller, Nate Crossland, Mike Bova, Lukas Ace, Norman McKay, Charlie Covington, Drew Crane, Blake Chapman, Parker McCown, Alex Anthony, RJ Martin, David Kobola, Craig Cosgrove; Carrie Robinson, Carolyn Fridley, Ally Milewich, Alex Winters, Emma Holman, Rachel Galloway, Grace Davis, Kristyl Lankford, Heather Michalak, Emma Groo, Olivia Lobdell, Sarah Sloan, Tara Romig, Christine Luu, Stephanie Gross; Brendan, Colin, and Molly Rice; Matt, J, Pat, Mandy, and the Crockett family; the W.T. Woodson Choral Department, Russell Gong, Michael Belovitch, Luke Savoca, Mia Savoca, Regan McLaughlin, Chris Lamore, Andrew Hain, Ben and Chris Marple, Brandon Fowlkes, Anthony Khong, Jeffrey Schwartz, Alvaro Aunon, Jose Fuentes, Shaquil Njovens, Kevin Über; Khalil Toure, Clay Rucker, Eric Cecchett, Arlie Bagley, Emma Maiorana, Anders Bruce, Caleb Brennan, Emily Cooper, Chase Kiddy, Sean Strang, Collin Rosenbluth, Davion Birdsong, Doug and Will Smith, Tyler and Spencer Gritis, Joe Cordes, Jesse Smith, Eain Cole, Eric Bernal, Ethan Todd, Gavin Philips, J Shuniak, Jaimie Appleton, Gabe Grant, Ben Grimes, Frankie Leonard, Tim Kinni, Zoe Weinstein, Danny Ryer, Bobby Shoemaker, Shelbi Fiddler, Josh Solomon and his family, Jordan Abreu, Julie Martin, Bob Edelman, Erica Winchester, Justin Briner, Kathryn Probus, Katie Keller; Lawson, Kyle, and Ted Gordon; Marisa Cagnoli, Maximillian Williams, Patrice Bird, Chantie Nguyen, Daniel Dechiara, Michael Bush, Michael Johnson, Nathan Gallagher, John Huffman, Pablo Cabrera, Dom Telle, Sam Gault, Kevin Costigan, Tim Bush; Taylor Hender and his family; Tom Sardo, Austin Carpenter, Bennett Wales, Michelle Mannino, John Mulhall, Kelly McCoy, Nolan Thornton, Joshua Tyree, Terry Glover, Naseer Conway, JMU, Harrisonburg's Downtown Books, the Whitehead family; Brian, Stephen, and the Murphy family; Walter, Emily, and the Gawlak family; Caitlin Connolly and her family; Michael Bush, Alex Smith, John Bachman, Michelle Cecchetti, Robert Mathis, Dillon Vita-Finzi, Kris Shy, Megan Makarowski, Megan Brothers, Kari Owens, Juliana Garabedian, Veronica Adams, Haylie Ahart, Traymon Beavers, Robert Fadley, and all the other amazing classmates I've had the pleasure of workshopping with; the teachers/professors/guitarists who encouraged me, including but not limited to: Patty Morris (who got me to write in the first place), Michael Ehrlich, Benjamin Horen, Daniel Flage, Sarah Brooks, Amy Paugh, Fletcher Linder, Hannah Kelley, Traci Zimmerman, Susan Ghiaciuc, Elisabeth Whitehead, Michael Smith, Heather Comfort, Laurie Kutchins, William Lawton, Samar Farah Fitzgerald, Shelley Aley, Cynthia Martin, Scott Lunsford, Alex Parrish, Ginger Moran, Jay Varner, Paul Bogard, Elden, Simon, and Koenig/Rau.

About the Author

Tommy Sheffield was born in 1991, in Fairfax, Virginia. He is currently an undergraduate at James Madison University, studying Writing, Rhetoric and Technical Communication. His work has been published in *Lexia*, *More than Medium*, *Gardy Loo*, and *Ming Magazine*.

Printed in the United States
By Bookmasters